THE SKINS OF POSSIBLE LIVES

by Renée Gregorio

Renée Gregorio

prints by Bill Gersh

BLINKING YELLOW BOOKS

Taos, New Mexico

ISBN 1-8839-6805-4

The "Caravans" Suite is reproduced with the permission
of the Bill Gersh Estate.
The titles of the individual prints are as follows:
cover: "Man on Woman's Head"
inside (in order of appearance): "Garden of Eden",
"Man is Wolf to Man", "Mayan Chants" and "Cloud Singers".

Author photo: John Brandi

The publishers would like to thank:
Gina Azzari, Rachel & Georgia Gersh, and S.O.M.O.S.

Blinking Yellow Books is a non-profit press
for the benefit of writers.
Contact us at: P.O. Box 1860
Ranchos de Taos, NM 87557
tel: (505) 751-4350

First printing: 1996

ACKNOWLEDGEMENTS

The author wishes to thank the editors of the following journals, where many of these poems first appeared.
"Partings" and "This Conversation Begins Amidst Order" appeared in *The Rialto*, Vol. 2, 1985, Norwich, England; "Stepfather's Trumpet" in *The New Mexico Humanities Review*, Vol. 8, No. 2, 1985, Socorro, NM; "Djuna Rearranged" in the *Exquisite Corpse*, Vol. 5, Nos. 9-12, 1987, Baton Rouge, LA; "Valentine" in *Fish Drum*, Issue No. 1, 1988, Santa Fe, NM; "Tracing Sources" in *The Taos Review*, Vol. 1, 1989, Taos, NM; "Marsha's Hieroglyphics" and "Shattering the Blind Corral" in *The Taos News Fall Arts Supplement*, 1989, Taos, NM; "Hunger for the Fox's Stance" (which appeared as "Hunger for a Stillness to Call Home") in *Kennebec*, Winter 1990, Augusta, ME; "Rushes" in *Prairie Smoke*, 1990, Pueblo, CO; "Silent Dialogue" in *Blue Mesa Review*, 1991, Albuquerque, NM; in *The New Mexico Poetry Renaissance*, Red Crane Books, 1994, and in *¡Saludos!*, Pennywhistle Press, 1995; "Sawing Till the Wood Sings" and "Virtues of Silence" in *the eleventh muse*, Colorado Springs, CO, 1991; "Marsha's Hieroglyphics" in *The Rialto*, Winter 1991; "Body without Limit" (which appeared as "Journey without a Plane Ticket") in *Nudes & Other Beauties*, Photosalon Usvara, Latvia, 1992; "Loose Change" in the *Exquisite Corpse*, No. 51, 1995.

Thanks also to the Millay Colony for the Arts in Austerlitz, NY for providing a residency, in which time this collection was organized and revised.

And final and biggest thank you to the daughters of Bill Gersh, Georgia and Rachel, who have granted permission to publish Gersh's prints in this book. Of course, thanks to Bill Gersh for his agreeing to do so before his death, for his art, for his love.

*to those who have
marked my life,
then moved on,
especially to Bill
and to Ken*

CONTENTS

TOWARD THE MOUNTAIN'S HEART

THE MOUTH, DRAWN OPEN

ENTERING THE CURRENT

BUILDING SONG

TOWARD THE MOUNTAIN'S HEART

MUSHROOM HUNTING

Amanita muscaria, the sound of your name
makes me see things. I saw you, speckled
and red-hooded, hiding behind the aspens.
The other hikers walked by; you were far in,
not easily visited from the rock-strewn path.
Something made me turn, walk toward the mountain's heart.
There were five of you, mottled but glowing,
like a dying fire. I'd no idea
what you were, but I picked you anyway,
ran off to show you to my friends. They said,
Oh how strange! and didn't know your name.
They were searching the white edibles,
mushrooms they knew were safe for soups.
I went where my feet said to go.
It hurt climbing to the high, wet country.
Poisonous with visions.

PARTINGS

In the end, they cannot make the crossing.
They're left on the harbor's edge,
waiting without schedules, without a weather report,
for a ship that would contain them.

His baggage weighed in too heavy, hers
not enough. The authorities denied them
passage, weighing all possibilities,
each coming up *No, we do not have the space you desire.*

She is weeping, she is weeping, and the soft shields
of her eyes are falling; she cannot see distances.
He is weeping, he is weeping under the glass
of his eyes, tinted to hide his profusion of tears.

They turn to each other. When once they would have
embraced, they can now only nod, reach out
a hand, feel the bones on the other's face,
turn again toward the wave's sudden swell.

CLAIMING THE INVISIBLE

In my dream, the ocean outside your door
didn't belong; it was too beautiful.
I said, *I don't remember this here.*
This isn't how it used to be.

What I hold most precious changes shape;
I'm afraid to relinquish all those other lives,
remembering the stitch in every shirt,
the voices of old men in pubs.
I can't release them. They live and breathe in my skin.

We were trying for that one
clear voice over the radio station,
passing back and forth across the Mexican border.
What grew between us, static-free.
But always the blazing fire in the distance,
the obliterated horizon.

Write your name on everything that's yours,
I hear a father tell his son. I should've written
my name across your skin, claimed it
like I used to claim a new schoolbook.
Write your name on everything you can, I say,
the kitchen sink, his left earlobe, the banks of the Rio Grande.

I was driving home on a single promise,
not considering whether it would be kept or not.
For love, we ate raw oysters with lemon,
let them slide down our throats without choking,
let the words out, careful to keep a secret,
not knowing love dies enshrined.

The demons are spreading their wings
against the backs of old photographs.
I wanted what was most severe in you,
what I couldn't name as my own.
I had thought a familiar face could tell me
something, that blur of unrealized hope.
What level of blindness has consumed me?
How is it that we continue at all?

RESIDENCES

1
The fear of loss is physical:
a child estranged in a museum
screaming for her mother, all
she knows, gone.
She stands still with her terror.

A child anywhere, a department-store basement,
separated from her parent, always
remembers that twist in her heart.
A woman watching her lover's hand trace the shape
of another woman's ass remembers her rage forever.
Her body remembers.

2
Roger smashes his paintings, wanting
to be just an ordinary person.
How can you be just an ordinary person
when what's inside is the hidden tongue,
simultaneous images of definition and destruction,
holding and letting go?

3
Remote and unyielding, this mountain life.
Staying is all there is, but lonely.
A puppet on very long strings, Hyland wrote.
The residences of our affair, she said to her lover.
The long waiting to arrive.

I'm caught in the tumbleweed.
I'm caught in the mountains.
I make laws for a kind of living;
I could fill the alphabet with exceptions.
Is the fascination really located in the imbalance?

4

Take all the faces in America
from behind their newspapers. Separate
from what aches in you: the persistent feeling
that everything could just disappear.

Goodbye to his shape, now forgotten. Goodbye
to his excesses, which entered me. I excrete him.
The cleverness of his knowing. His stupidity.
His dreams wed to his cowardice.
Goodbye to our urgency. Our lies.

Again, from nothing, I begin.

VIRTUES OF SILENCE

Words echo in departure's undertow.
Apologies take a year, from one continent
to the next, another figure beyond the whitened
mountains, alone on a mesa, her hair blown back
like a witch's hair in flight, a figure with memories
of soundproof glass rising as she walked toward the gate.
A thin voice gets through, disembodied.
An unspoken, unlived forgiveness.

There are messages that arrive late or not at all.
Long after the gossip is gone, after every scent goes
from the trailer, from my mouth, goes from the blue
corduroy shirt and the brown leather vest,
when the scent of cactus and mushrooms goes
and what we saw in the Arizona desert,
the shadows at sunset, how you imagined them to be men.

Voices linger. Accents with fire in them echo
down a dark, empty corridor I almost forget.
I almost forget telephone poles in Islington,
how what you knew ran over me like water's relief.

Your sweat is in the rim of your hat.
The single red rose with its broken stem wilts.
Everything is a tiny memory on some part of the skin.
I remember the pureness at desire's core.

LOOSE CHANGE

How to manage this correspondence,
or any, for that matter.
Leaving without sign or signature,
a hand pushed into concrete before it dries.
Yet another set of unlived possibilities,
a sudden hailstorm just as suddenly over.
Imprints, sketches on the underside of skin,
words etched into new places, refusing
to accept the impossibility of anything.
There's nothing but sagebrush here;
what was once ocean turning forever
into its absence, but the air still breathes salt.
Nothing much lasts, not even this absence
in its present form. But some decisions
are definite, knife-slicing, full of blood.
And in all that red, all the daring to refuse.
Perhaps nothing lasts. But there's still
seventy-two cents worth of loose change
on the carpet, and a few feathers
from a dead, red-breasted bird
the cat dragged in before they made love.

ECHO AMPHITHEATER

Water marks spill down the rock-face,
deep red on pale orange, spidery dried blood.
This theater's a bowl of sound,
a ship of air. The horizon's upward: a wave-
cloud through blue, trees erupting from stone,
the earth's boundaries raw, untenable.

All voice is an echo, all sound a stoney return.
Too many shouting at once ends in babble,
the obscure danger behind a siren's wail.
Short, sharp sounds echo best, the sign says.
A leaf's softer turning doesn't reverberate.
Here's a stage for word's re-making.
An unoriginal theater giving back
piercing sounds, the brief masks of voice.

THIS CONVERSATION BEGINS AMIDST ORDER

She's walked these streets
alone for months.

She sends him out of her room
with his shaving gear.
He asks: can I leave my sweater?
She agrees.

(She dreams of pushing the light switch on.
Nothing happens.
In the dark room,
drunks in soiled overcoats
on benches with bag-ladies.

She pushes the light switch off.
She doesn't know where to go.)

In the rainy street,
he looks behind himself.
Is she there?
Is anyone?
She approaches, running.

Together, they board the bus.
Thin-lipped wives
with stiff and straw-dry hair
read the newsprint they embrace
with bony, ringed fingers.

(He dreams of protecting a woman,
of getting stabbed, over and over.)

She wakes from dreaming he's crying,
as he asks in the twilight,
did you dream I was crying?

She leans out, just to see
where the birds fly
with such black-winged speed,
such fierce alacrity.

THE RULES OF WINTER

There is danger, the scent of it on the snowy path,
in the quickly darkening sky, the sense of it
in a memory of disappearance, the sudden barrenness
of a room emptied of its lovers.

Cold comes through the glass like someone speaking
a horrible truth in a whisper,
an eerie presence, an odd harkening. Transported
into a fiery realm that's foreign, sharp.

All continuity's ablaze. There's some song I keep turning to,
a song I keep wanting to turn. I dreamed you
were Amadeus and I straddled the arms of the chair.
You laughed. All I really wanted was the laughter.

Its making and un-making. Its center and periphery.
Here, I let things be without roses or rawness.
The leaf releases itself from the tree.
A single star reaches through the skylight: pulsing   pulsing.

JESSICA'S POEMS

I. Jessica's Visitations

An unknown bed in the afternoon,
light shifting through thin, white curtains,
candle emitting its ancient gold.

What is she doing here? The man long gone,
the void, black and unfathomable, her inescapable
haunting. The long, slow process of speaking her mind.

This bed isn't hers. This bed is only half his.
She listens to the intermittent traffic in the street below,
listens for car doors, footsteps, another woman's voice.

II. Jessica Knife-Catching

She's catching knives now,
their absolute corners of sharpness.
They fall off counters as she washes
the dishes. She moves fast,
barely containing her grasp over edges,
meeting the knife-tip just in time.
She never gets cut up,
thick-skinned and bloodless,
never gets hurt, never cries,
her gaze always just beyond
the last mountain.

III. Fragments of her Old Name

She hated mirrors, stuck her tongue out at herself
as she passed. Once, in the dark, she threw
a bowl at the only mirror in her house.
Reflections bore down on her.

Walking through broken glass, a thousand images
of herself emerging, her private nightmare.

Years later, she renamed herself *Jessica.*
She lost the sound of her birth-name,
wandered the streets searching for what once rooted her,
some familiar tone or spelling or scent of that first identity.

IV. Jessica Remembers

Her father in a wheelchair. Her father
with his crooked eyes. Her father
alone, talking of his life: a trip
around the world in a ship that sank.

She looked at him after all these years
of not knowing him. She looked hard and long,
amazed to see herself in his eyes,
an odd sort of mirror, deep recognition.

Nearly half her life over, spent healing
unnecessary wounds. She's roamed too much
in the reckless part of herself, annihilating
everything she's come to call her own.

Like wind raging, like lightning,
as if running from the law,
as if she's doing everything for the last time,
a mad rush of sensation, a bridge's underbelly.

She knows the scent of doorways as the city darkens.
She wants to name the body whose shadow is there.
What a nightmare to wake up and realize you're anyone.
She wants to wake in awe of a gift clearly given.

V. Naming the Dark

He said: *Jessica, I fell down the basement stairs*
at some party of candles. I don't remember
much else. Jessica thought: he gets angry
when no one speaks to him in the morning.
What he can't remember couldn't have entered
his heart. The juggler with all his tricks
falling to the ground.

What isn't heard under that particular slant
of light in darkness? What isn't seen or felt there?

She wanted to remember
the strand of black hair caught in the wood's grain.
Running through the megaliths, his fingers
pointing down the ancient row of stones.

She couldn't go anywhere, woman with a black
gate covering her face, woman with cages in her eyes.

VI. Jessica's Paraphernalia

Someone's dream contains a white picket fence.
Not Jessica's. Jessica dreams of Dennis Hopper's
baggy grey suit receding down a brick corridor
in a back alley of Santa Fe. She dreams
of heavy threads, impenetrable flaws
in her fabric. She dreams of shedding, a deep
drenching in the undiscriminating air.
Not the language of sleep, but some new words
for waking, no more shapeless, suspended voices.

Soot-filled city windows, unfamiliar faces
on unknown streets, the train's wail in the night,
her body running under bridges in the rain—
all this the paraphernalia of her night-life—
Sometimes she dreams completed things: a child
fully formed, a finished poem on its page.

Dreaming on the edge of last words, he said to her:
Don't forget that little thing in you. She said:
Don't forget anything. What to say when there's
only one chance? Ecstasy, not duty.
Reframing the noise into intelligent song.

VII. Passageways to Jessica

Nothing stays the same here. Not the arrangement of furniture
or paintings on the walls, not the bedsheets or the order of books
on their shelves, not the shelves or the window's cleanliness,
or the morning cries of birds, or the disposition of cells.
Jessica's cleaning dust and worms out of the corner of her rooms.

Sometimes the smells just aren't right:
too much blood, too much scent of woman
in the carpet, too much residue of smoke,
empty bottles, conversations left on the edge,
the wilderness just about to be entered,
the desperation finally admitted.

She has to keep knocking at the door
of the house she's lived in for years.
The weeds in the garden are ragged edges of cloth.
She can't tell what's blossoming from what's wilting.

These are first steps in a long chain of rearranging
this long line of shattering. Other winds become
barely imaginable. Her heart runs on winter
in this house, stacking and re-stacking the wood.

VIII. Jessica's Ascent

Just east of the earth's tremendous rift,
its massive fault, just east of the earth's aching,
the walking rain forms its distant screen,
an illusory wall. There were sounds he knew;
she wants to make them her own—
sirens and whistles, wind and leaves,
the sensual mumbling of lovers
through hotel walls. A secret,
deeper pulse. A sudden brilliance.

She will throw away the reckless, fragmented
letters; she has no use for them.
She knew him when he forgot
his cowardice. You will find her still
hunting the long, untrodden path,
forgetting, then remembering,
her name.

IX. Living in Two Countries

From the abnormally large chair where it hung,
she tears down the sign bearing his name.
A life fills in around this absence.
It's fall and everything's ripe and ready to shed.

It's another woman's face she wakes with.
Someone he walked off with once. Slept in the woods with once.
Years later she wakes with this memory.
She wakes with this woman since he is already up and gone,
wakes wondering why he did this and what it was like.

Sometimes hands can reach across absence, foreign
countries, other lovers, can awaken a forgotten,
familiar sensation under the skin, a human spring.
Other times all is unyielding, driving through
mountain roads in a snowstorm when winter breaks.

In a neighborhood of whores and music students,
she found herself tied to herself in an unfinished room
on a quiet street the traffic didn't reach. Odd to see
her there alone with all those empty rooms.
She entered the morning air with a new way of naming things.

Having lived in two countries, she finds it impossible to live
in one again. The stories she tells of the other place
don't help. Because no one can know the sense her foot has
of stepping on two streets at once, or how rain and urine
can evoke two cities simultaneously.

Often, we are elsewhere or not ourselves.
Maybe it is possible to dream the other life back.
She is alone now, waking to the vivid mirror-image
of a man she once knew. She enters the mirror,
faces what she cannot hold as her own.

THE MOUTH, DRAWN OPEN

FOLLOWING THE KICKBALL

Mrs. MacHugh used to spell secrets
to my grandmother. I always knew the words.
Someone left. The long disappearance of footfall,
an empty corridor where the step's sound
breaks the vacuum, defies natural law.

My family is a constellation. The individual
stars are harder to make out over distance.
Silhouetted in doorways, the patriarchal aura
of my grandfather. There's always my mother
standing there, too, saying goodbye again.

She must've climbed the long hill
of Prospect Street, her child tight
to her chest, the two-story green
clapboard house emptied behind her,
the child's heart touching her own.

When I was a kid, I'd take my grandfather's
shoes off over his brown, gout-swelled ankles.
I'd unravel my grandmother's good silver
wrapped in thick plastic under starched,
white napkins. Now, over a telephone,
I hear a strange old woman's voice call to her
from hospital bed to hospital bed.
I am far away again as she tells me:
Everything's changed now.

The light shifts faster than I can follow it.
I remember the little red schoolhouse,
the sharp incline at the back of the playing field,
how the red kickball always tumbled between trees,
making its swift descent into the deeper woods.

CIRCA 1958

the silver container
the flash bulb holds
reflects a portion of the sun
a man's arm
around a little girl's waist
he is kneeling
his khaki jacket shines a little
she might believe
he is handsome if she had eyes
to look at him that way
but she is a child dressed for Easter
anyway her eyes are shut
he is clutching her navy blue coat
at what will be a woman's hip one day
she is leaning   back arched against
the air   a smile printed
on her chubby face
the tree limbs at the top
of the frame hang tentatively
over the white trellis
wisps of a child's hair
not the real thing
the tree trunk entirely
out of view.

TRACING SOURCES

On conversation's edge, there's a lie
we've yet to tell each other. Or a truth.
This voice is strange. Listen
to the spaces between words.

What mouth brings these sounds
clear across the country?
What face belongs to this mouth?
What body attaches itself to this face?
What right, love?
What language?

Silence, a burning speech
that's never been enough, Father.
Years of forming the word
for you with tentative tongue,
years of missing you.
Now there's a real voice on the wires,
found, resurrected, delivered across
the intimate spaces of two lifetimes.

Two syllables. To fill
the word with breath,
to breathe life into its soft vowels,
to claim it as vocabulary.

All of this is enough, for now.
Old enough to make friends, Pound said.
One root, tired of brokenness.
Perhaps there is room for commerce.

STEPFATHER'S TRUMPET

You used to play in the basement
on Saturday afternoons, the windows clamped down,
so not to disturb the neighbors, and you wouldn't
play long, so not to disturb the people inside the windows.

For years, I didn't see you
play, only heard the sharp thrill of your
loud notes, echoing up the stairway,
pulsing down the walls to my bedroom.

You didn't practice often. Once in a while
you'd stand by my piano bench and snap
your fingers, a metronome I couldn't
keep time to. And you'd chant: practice practice.

Or you'd shout from the other room when I
slipped up, missed a beat. It threw me
off. Our rhythms didn't match. How
could I tell you this; how could we perform?

I don't play piano anymore. And you
never practice at home. You meet your musician
friends in empty halls, blow your golden horn
for hours, stamping your foot to your own rhythm.

Once, I saw you rehearse in the back room
of a Chinese restaurant. You stood to play a solo.
My head ached for wanting to cry
as I finally felt a piece of song rise from your throat.

BORDER TOWN

Passage, marked by a falling-down sign,
crumbling adobes, the want for elsewhere
just because it's there. My father's eyes
eventually looked off in two different directions.
Always, the imagining of another life.
After everyone goes, the fresh scent of abandonment—
a new cut on the skin, a blister from raking,
the shedding of all that's useless.
What's underneath is skin, the endless organ,
regenerating. Snake-like, I have shed myself
on many layers of the earth's surface. The woman
I left standing at the airport has taken another flight;
she's disappeared, lives somewhere in a city.
Memory's image quiets itself, withers.
What is it to know arrival? Yes, I can breathe.
And there are connections to be made, some
too brief. The desperation dissipates.
Change happens. I scatter my energy between the absence
of light and the coming of light. I abandon myself
to the passage, as if the answers were always
just floating in the river.

LANDSCAPE WITH SMOKE

Mist hangs in the distance
where roads stop and valley
is a gaping mouth without speech,
is a woman's inner thighs,
is a child's willingness to laugh.
Across the mesa,
the mountain's faraway outline,
a faint pencil sketch on the western horizon,
a backdrop, hardly believable.
The rainbow is split; streaks
of rosy smoke in the silence,
all color just out of reach.
What was once short, bright shocks
of yellow across the mesa, all bitten
by early frost now, hay-dry and golden.
In sound's absence, the ears attend,
wind nearly cursing across sagebrush,
always a speech waiting to form
this earth's cracked shell of desert.
When clouds crawl in before sunrise,
mountains disappear. In this terrible absence,
the village is lost, unanchored,
drifting without boundary.
What makes good music:
the inevitable shift
from stacatto to legato,
the movement of sound on skin,
the shivering.

THE DIVER

for a painting by the same name
by Bill Gersh

He dives into a wounded sea.
Perched briefly at water's edge,
his hands, more like shovels,
balance there. As if water
were thick panes of immovable glass,
as if it were fixed, unbreakable,
something he gazes into, but cannot
penetrate. Black abyss that falls
off the edge of the picture-frame,
a place he knows little of.

Diver began his pink-bodied motion
in a dark sky streaming with occasional
streaks of blue. Began with the intention
of diving clear and strong into the sea.
Now he has turned acrobat, eternally
lingering just above water's brittle crest,
his head cocked as if to listen
to dark sounds beyond water's frame,
wanting immersion—shifting, wavering,
dancing on his hands, in fear of it.

EVERY WOMAN, AN ISLAND

On this very large island we call a continent,
I'm missing a missed connection. There's room
for the river's crazed meandering, room for the ocean
I can't see to rise and fall, swallowing images
I can no longer fathom, though they were once mine.

Is it an act of love if there's obliteration,
every touch leading you farther away from yourself ?
I want to poke a finger into the unseen.
The far sea's cry follows my dreaming,
what's not possible, always tickling.

I don't know what's possible without a scar.
I would want to be allowed to walk away unscathed.
But there's always something: the child's head
ripping the mother's flesh, the years of scrapes
on playgrounds, the angled slash of an appendectomy.

My mouth is drawn open to language I haven't learned yet,
all of me hopeful, like a healed scar. Yearning
is the clear pool at the bottom of the last hill
we can't seem to get to. Maybe we could climb to the top,
stare down into it like a dog panting over a puddle.
I would stare quietly. I would let it be.
Some places are meant to be left alone.

IT'S RAINING IN AUGUSTA

I'm drawn to the harsher seasons,
wind blasting against my chest,
against each grain of wood I clutch.
I want to pare it all down to nothing,
eliminate worn pieces of cloth from my wardrobe,
swim eroding banks by the old river,
silence the voices that speak in my ears,
invent in silence. But some days I'm caught
in my own skin; there's nowhere to go.
Somewhere, on the other side of the earth,
a man grows old without me, disintegrates.
I dream of him with a severed arm.
Sex was part of everything: the zoo,
the dog's life, the way he splashed words
on an empty page, the shiver from wind,
his heavy yawn. Everything. Now,
I carry the priest's voice at confirmation,
asking *what is pious?* I carry the scent
of incense in the Catholic Church. The black
wrought iron railing crawls on my back,
his hands under my shirt. I wanted anonymity,
to be part of the slur of people
crowding down the stairs at Euston Station.
Instead, I carry the imprint of hotel names,
the remembered desire for my skin,
a fragile green bird with red wings.
I left a scent of French perfume in the white rooms.
I left silence, so they could listen to themselves.
I left pulsing veins, a leaf with its own boundary.

GHAZAL FOR A SHIFTING LANDSCAPE

I've a paper boat,
but how to reach my destination in it?

It's OK. As long as you leave
fragrance behind you for a thousand years.

In Bisbee, a strange man beckoned,
mistaking her for a dancer.

This day is full of beasts: the tarantula's slow crawl
on adobe, the lizard's flight from what's invisible.

Magpies glide in front of the window,
light and shadow delicately balanced.

A glove too small
is a terrifying thing.

FRAGMENTS OF THE HEART

In the dreaming body
where we were or will be
another jungle leaks
under skin another threshold
in another doorway a note
a dark scar far away
an attack of the heart
in the water of my dreams
other men twins
unspeakable fire
railroad tracks take you
back lead you forward
self giving birth to self
the final scar on the flesh

ENTERING THE CURRENT

NOT A TRADITION

Who would not have wished
something to come of it?
Something to come of the afternoons
thick with bitter beer, climbing up
and down stairwells to the canal?
Who doesn't wish for continuation?
I'd bet the borage still grows in his garden.
I'd bet the webs still sew the wood beams
together, his desire for connection.
I was hoping for a time herb,
like the dock leaf, that heals
the sting of backing into nettles.
I find no such herb. I remember
his dream of two plants connected
at the root. He woke and told me so.
Who would not have wished
something to come of it?
Sodo alchemica. I name the work
we did together. In this territory,
only vultures glide. Roadrunners
move haltingly. So do rabbits.
They stop stupidly at the oncoming light,
hoping it's there to show them a way home.

DISJUNCTIONS

waking to a long, deep going.
disastrato, the Greeks say,
torn away from the stars.

she re-maps her journey to him,
falls into deeper sleep,
as he's just waking from morning's
first dreams, zones away.

some kind of fox,
some kind of hunter,
running the mountain's open spaces,
his silver cries choked
in the valley's eerie silence.

he moves beyond the mountains,
shape-shifting, coat turning to gray,
his journey folding in on itself,
a dead bird's wing.

A MAN WHO THINKS HE'S A FOX ESCAPES WEST

At first Taos presented the kind of man
you'd meet in the express line at the supermarket,
the kind who can't stop smiling,
who gives himself only one name
and it sounds like *ease,*
who parts saying *see you on the road.*

In search of an order never written down,
his outstretched arms each touched its own star.
She said she's done with the habit of suffering.

All that's really necessary: singing and sex,
and a choice of underwear in the morning.
A man announces: *I'm interested in other junctions,*
and everyone knew he meant her thighs.

She gave up writing poetry in a 3-piece suit,
spent time with people who were too normal to write,
so they drank, gave that up and wrote so she wouldn't drink.

Front is where the legs bend, that's all.
I have to call information to get my birthfather's number.
I read the headlines: "A Man Who Thinks He's a Fox Escapes West."
I guess it's time to be in the business of acquiring keys.

That man who thought he was a fox said to me:
*I've been thinking. Either I ought to get a business
and hire you, or get a divorce and marry you.*
He did neither.

HEBRIDEAN LIGHT

Words and rivers. The full moon's breath
swelling the window-pane. No names

for this. Nothing to call a beginning.
A future of surprise visits, spontaneous calculations.

He calls her name. He calls it again.
His cry wakes her name to her cry.

Silence. The language of eruption.
She stares at the walls. He sweeps the crevices.

DJUNA REARRANGED

Your words turn wax-work figures
into live policemen; knotted characters without
choice of destiny stand all over the world,
close to the wall. Children, desperadoes,
no volition for refusal. Nora had the face,
her provision of herself. Robin stayed with her
until they descended. *Don't wait for me,*
she said. Their subsequent gestures of abandon
on the narrow iron bed brought thoughts of acorns,
roadways...their bones ached out fire,
ponderable hair, mighty uncertainties,
blind searchlights of the heart.
I've got to write what leaves
a memory of its weight, she said. Nothing
to go by to make broken hearts whole.

MEASURING THE DISTANCE

The distance between her lovers' beds
is a wrench, a scythe, a hammer, a rake and hoe.
The distance, a hair's breadth, a wolf's face,
a shimmering robe, a sheet's thickness. The distance
is familiar like the space between the twin beds of brothers.
The sound of rain on adobe or the constant drip
from a tiny leak in the ceiling evoke this distance.
It is a black key caught down a thin hole.

You have to face the underside of everything, lived with
or tasted. There's a terror in giving the self away,
a fish caught at the end of its hook. I remember
the strength of what was then passing swiftly between us,
the rawness at the center, the daring to begin.
In an unrooted world, a slightly shocked fervor
runs in the animal-scented air.

I dream of sleeping in an old apartment that was once mine.
I was afraid to sleep in someone else's place,
even though I had the key. I want memory to be
without aching. I build correspondences.
What will I say to the woods and the stalks of corn?

He didn't want explanations or fever,
didn't want her lips or confessions,
or to remember falling asleep in her bed,
or waking with terror at an open window.

It's embarrassing to be in one place for too long,
but what's too long, and who's noticing?

Intelligent choice is exquisite torture.

YELLOW SPRING

This season shapes itself around
windchimes, vessels, old bird's nests, string.
Everything seems on the edge of working.
In the yard, a man gathers
the earth's gnarled branches, roots.

What must fall away, does. What burns
leaves a patch of black on the earth,
a reminder that something's died here.
It doesn't take long for the new growth to enter.
Oblivion comes and goes. I forget fearing nothing lasts.

Once, I knew a man who made webs.
He'd just sit for hours with string and a tree,
playing a spider's game. He made webs
from East London to the Sangre de Cristos;
his fingers' whisper echoes.

The river goes by anyway, with its piece
of broken-off log, swirling. All that has seemed
necessary will be laughable one day. Hope
has been the fugitive. It is now the river
I drown in.

BODY WITHOUT LIMIT

the words went first
though in every other normal day
the words were most crucial.
they went flickering into the primitive
cave called fireplace, drawn to the uplift
of air, drawn on fire's wings, fire's tendrils,
sinewy as light in night-photography,
long waves in a black hole,
accepting light.

it was the skin that went next,
organ of boundary that meets the air's
shafts at every corner,
claims hold on the entire body.
this definition left, skin becoming
more wave-like than wall, body
without limit's shape.

the ears suddenly heard the sea
as if from a shell, though the body
was inland. and the hands went numb,
fell to the floor, no longer
needing to touch. it was something
far beyond skin, bones, blood
that grasped at the air, a new sense,
seeing in slower patterns, till what stayed
was the sharp sting of being as alive
as the flagstones under body,
as the mud in these walls.

WEDDING

We've been in stillness training for years now,
squatting at the river's edge, naming each piece of bark.
Once we were girls who asked the same questions,
misbehaved and giggled afterwards. As women we met
in foreign countries, found the *goodbye* of one back, retreating.

Here I turn manure into soil, make a fertile place to begin.
There's plenty of room for the vegetables.
Oceans rise and fall even if I'm not there to see.
Johanna, it was you who said *I'm done with the habit of suffering.*
Searching heart's ease, you came to this intersection.
Now shimmer, glide, explode. Own the wider vision of forests.

Love requires remembering, I'd swear to it.
Every touch leads you back to the source of the river,
then forward, imagining the final spill into oblivion,
or the Atlantic. Turn and twist in the sheet's stillness,
till you find your own brief stillness. Everything
is within reach now. The haunting disappears.

Enter the current without boat or paddle.
Search the hidden, the marrow, the beacon in the distance.
There are no paths, only the opportunity for continuance.
Let yourself be taken far out of yourself, where the stars are
only beginning to show their light.

RUSHES

Mostly, I want to go to sleep
realizing there is love in my life,
and then I want to stop dreaming
of houses I don't live in except in dreams—
perfect and singular, with more rooms
than I'd ever need.
I want to throw away my old things,
start again from nothing, rearrange
my cells in the shape of birds of paradise,
or blue irises or the sound of blues or the taste
of olive oil on anchovies or I want to feel
like a mirror does or a black hole
or the long shimmering journey of a falling star.

I really only want to be something other than I am.
Doesn't everybody? The blues. If she'd take me back.
If he'd take me back. If we never let go. Walk away.
Just walk away. Everyone tries to until one day, one night,
you simply can't and staying is all there is, bodies fusing
under the wide night sky. Obliterate the blues?
Impossible.

The night is as restless as we'll let it be.
You can run the streets and bars looking
for love or something like it, or not.
The madness of living with all that is possible,
afraid of disappearing without boundary.
But there are seconds when the gods meet in the air
between two faces, when all is believed in.
This morning's sunlight pulsates
in the cleft of the aloe leaves.

Trying on the skins of possible lives,
years came together, years went away.
One learns to live in the immediate jungle,
planting gardens at every turn, letting
the grass grow unwieldy. There isn't as much time
as you think, isn't much time at all.
Kissing at dusk in an unknown doorway.
Kissing anywhere. His hand rests
on the black silk of her leg, as he lifts it away,
his handprint etched into the silk.

Closets within closets. The earth under rocks.
Shadows. What resides there? What goes on
in a darkened room when no one's in it
and all the doors are locked?

Concentrating on the shift in every cell.
Thinking of falcons, how they hover in perfect stillness
above their prey, how startling to watch their waiting,
simply waiting. The absolute patience of their maneuvering.
Their inner timing. The corners of his eyes.
That gnawing at the edges. Heat rising from groin.
I keep seeing the falcons. The wildness of edges.
Straining towards the light like the wandering jew
in the dark corner of my kitchen.

The memory of the New York skyline across the Hudson.
I'd look at the skyline and think of you,
how you were always just out of reach, always perfect
and defined and distant as those high rises, reaching
across water I couldn't travel. How incredible it is to make love
to a man who doesn't mind blood. In the next breath,
the knowledge that nothing is about endings.
At times there's nothing beyond skin touching, tongues
finding each other. Let's hear it for the scent of strangeness,
the forbidden, the difficult, the rich, the strong,
the largeness of his body, an accent unlike my own.

Once, I thought I would stay in the north of England,
some border town on an island, living with a man
who all his life carried the name of another man.
But I couldn't bear the thought's weight, never sure
of the words that sprang green and full of hope
from his British lips. Caught in the word's absolute bareness,
he lived, over and over, in the stories he created of himself.
I had to go from him. He had difficulty recognizing himself
in a mirror. The banshee's keening reached across
the border from Scotland, her wail without shape,
haunting the landscape. I wanted him to touch
the blood on the prison wall's grafitti, to feel the demons
residing there. I woke to the same startling window,
opening to tears. Which one lasts through the other's
changing? Gone, as they all are, into the silence,
a part of the air we breathe.

BUILDING SONG

SAWING TILL THE WOOD SINGS

At first, the hand aches,
saw weighing on tensed muscle,
fingers seized on metal,
a grip that sets her teeth grating.
Back and forth, the long serrated blade
grinds the old cedar posts, useless
for anything but burning.
Then slowly, the loosening of her grasp,
letting the tool at hand do its work,
her vigor simply guiding it
over the wood's irregular surface.
The sound of her labor shifts.
Her face muscles relax, teeth unclench,
then, as if to answer her with her own unfamiliar song,
the wood whispers, the saw echoes its own cry,
and together—her strength, the aging wood, the metal tool—
are synchronized, wholly working,
uttering a strain she imagined once,
but never heard.

MARSHA'S HIEROGLYPHICS

1

No memory. The world is blank.
She sits with her brush stroke, waiting
for the empty mind, her hand knowing where
on the canvas, the hand's release, a shiver,
one final explosion that tells all,
that is both empty and full. No memory
lives in her brush stroke. Or all memory.

2

I don't know anything that's true,
anything that's false. I don't know
if sound exists without an ear,
or if anything at all exists
except what we make so. This season is harsh.
I sleep a lot. Every move I make combs
past and present; what's left is raw, like earth
under dead leaves. Every cell has its own memory.

I carry wood from the pile in the yard
to the shelter of home. I turn each piece over,
remembering the folds in my grandmother's neck,
the rage in my mother's throat. I am not sad
or happy. I hold the wood tight to my chest.

3

She says yes, and the snow melts.
She says yes, and the sky empties.
She says yes, and the season opens around her,
a ripe peach splitting. She says yes.

BIRD-DEATH

I beat your heart. What never gets said leaks
off the tip of this pen, out the strands in your paintbrush.
What never gets said is the next blotch of red
in a strange woman's crotch, is the next face
with huge aqua-eyes and a spiked tongue.
For me, what doesn't hit the airwaves festers,
explodes here, quiets. I don't want to wake
in a fever of explanations. I want your will
to break my silence. I dream of return to forgotten
things, the river's severe wind to its source,
the rightness in the heart that drew us together.
I refuse silence. Do you know how the river
winds in excruciating twists to its source? The fish
are hunted. Trust is the slow center.
I bury my father's strangeness. I enter
a chamber without sounds. The morning's fever
takes me, then is gone. The question of death
is a bird's thump on the window. The sound
is too soft, too cushioned, its dying swings
like a badly hinged door in the wind.

LETTER TO THE HEART OF MY FAR COUNTRY

You're like them, with your strangling hands,
your smoky breath. You're like the prisoners
you teach, your hands killing, refusing
to move pen across page, address an envelope,
my name emblazoned on its front.
You strangle what you once loved,
the corpse stretched out in front of you.
You trip on my corpse, don't you?
But I'm not dead.

I read your poetry for messages from you.
I read *no, don't you ever come see me.*
I can hear your voice whispering hoarsely in my ear.

The dark surrounds us. I don't know where we are.
Energy changes hands. Can we meet where no one can see?
I want something tangible from you; even a stone
with a hole in it would do. I want to ask:
Is forgetfulness necessary for survival?

I'm not convinced. I'm crazy with your voice in my blood.
It's dug out of the earth like that sculpture in Thoreau;
the carved holes invite me in. I crawl into one's dark shape.
You're next to me in another hole.
We burrow and scrape; the walls won't give way.
I scratch the surface of what contains you.

I know the numbered buses of your city, their routes
and timetables. I think of the roads you travel, wonder
where you go. Is it anywhere? Or just further
into your own grief, the grief you name a prisoner's?
I live on the side of a mountain. I am rooted in this earth.
You didn't let me say goodbye.

I imagine slipping away from you,
saying one final line, watching curtains fall.
I walk off stage, the rigid grip of last words
in my jaw. I release the memory of you from the center
of what I've become, change costumes, walk down that city street
unrecognizable, without my former name, without speech.

What was open closed suddenly, a door in a windstorm.
I didn't know it was coming.
For months, I looked for you on the mesa; I wanted you back.
I'd stretch out on the earth and stare at the sky.
Its largeness was all that could hold me. Its endlessness.
I would've died in that city.

Now, I'll look for you in the open, not to resurrect you,
but to make sure you exist. I doubt our exchange.
I would like to sit across a table from you and talk,
see the new lines on your face,
the sour way you could look. I would like to hear
your accent when you say *love*,
reach across the empty space,
connect my hand with yours, dare to look you in the eyes,
not have you turn away. Yes,
I'm out on the desert walking,
and I'm headed in your solitary direction.
I must know who you are without me.

HUNGER FOR THE FOX'S STANCE

What is there to enter anymore?
Oblivion stopped working. I want to crawl
inside his one blind eye, make it right,
give him peripheral vision,
center vision, strength to see.
It was just another day, fishing
in New Hampshire, just an easy day
floating on a pond, his fishline deep
in the water, deep into a tree trunk,
deep into the eye, piercing the retina.
If it'd hit his temple he'd be dead,
they speculated. I'd rather it'd hit a magpie
flying by. Instead, my brother's now half-blind.

In Islington, a blind voice teacher
taught me how to roar. We pretended to be picking
at the earth, our bodies rising and falling.
In this act of toil, she had us release
our voices; odd chants fell between floorboards.

Years ago, I let go of the act of eating
two dozen chocolate chip cookies to satisfy
an impossible hunger. Now, my hunger is for the fox's
stance, his camoflage and waiting. From a train window,
I see a fox stop suddenly, stare only at me.
I watch him run down the empty road,
realizing it's one I'll never press my foot against.
I envy his fur that changes color, his power
of observation, his decisiveness. I want his skin
over mine, the landscape entering me as beast.

At 18, I wanted to kill myself on the library steps,
in the rain, over my first lover. I'd hurt him.
I couldn't see how to go on. A god of righteousness
ruled over me. I'd never go to heaven. I'd go to purgatory.
Or maybe even hell. I ran from the girl in me
who slapped stickers on a perfect white house on Halloween.

But she wanted attention. She caught up with me
in the corridors of the English department. She flirted
with married professors. She wanted several lives at once,
foreign cities, many lovers. She wanted to catch the end
of the red silk scarf she saw rounding distant corners,
to own the body whose perfume spilled into strangers' compartments.

Her appetites were severe. She said *goodbye* often,
never believing *forever*. When silence at last consumed her,
all she wanted was to be informed when each of her ex-lovers died.
Line after line, I resurrect you, she would write.
Then ask herself, but from what death? Then one day
she said, *I will save nothing from its own destruction,*
and she became clear again. The old remembered scenes
became static as photographs in frames.

The stopped train is waiting for the proper signal
to begin again its familiar journey. Passengers only get
a peripheral view of the train's meandering.
You've got to walk to get it straight on. Or be the driver.
Peripheral vision is like basil in tomato sauce. It fills the gaps.
I'm after what's head-on, the single light burning
at the top of the stairs, inviting you to claim what's home.

SHATTERING THE BLIND CORRAL

I thought I heard water of the *acequia*
running at my feet. But I grasped
a handful of earth and it turned to dust
in my palm. The wind drove fine specks
of cottonwood past my window.
Has the desert's speech evolved, at last, to this?

Horror in my throat, a fist of unspoken words.
I could feel only terror at everything I may
have forgotten to feel. The curtain blows slowly
into the room, then slowly out over the cracked earth.
I'm not thinking of sex at all. I hear the telephone
ring in an empty house. No one will answer.

I'm thinking of transplanting, how delicate
the petunias looked in the raked earth.
One by one, I banged the base of each
green plastic pot till the roots gave way
and the tiny plant fell out in my hand.
The crime, as always, is forgetting this.

Tired of blind corrals, being driven there.
The gasp before I knew the direction
was mine, and the shivering afterwards.
It was a corral like any other.
I'd thought it had to do with gathering, not death.

Riding through Kansas, the dirt roads stretched out
for more miles than I'd like to travel,
stretched out like open questions. Occasionally,
a farm house with a clump of dead trees,
then sudden barrenness again. In the kitchen, we leave
a woman and a man behind making breakfast.

It's a radical act, marriage, my friend announced.
I'm searching for the muse's quarters, and I feel
like the hunted. Addicted to ceilings, the infinite space
in an adobe wall, the clarity of the western horizon.
I can't turn away. I've found a tiny foreign spot
on the soil of my birth. I pull frozen objects out of the earth.

VALENTINE

It's the breath I want from you
night after night in whatever bed
we find   the breath   that comes
and goes from your mouth into
my ear   my hair   as if
all night you're telling me a story
without end   and I am taking in
what makes you live, what's
killing you. It's your breath
I can't live without, your breathing
that makes its way into me
those moments like crystals
you said   and crystals are real.
It's the passion I'm after
the opening to our breathing together
the sound of your breath
reverberating through my head
your hands grabbing me in the dark
as if to say: *no you don't have to go*
the memory of your lips on my hair
your fingers running through each
strand of black.

SILENT DIALOGUE

You want to be free of so many things,
yourself for one. And the heavy vigas.
You want to be free of the driving wind,
the empty canvas, the wilting strawberry plants.

I don't know how to walk here, among the ruins.
I trip on the rough-edged stones. It's too dry;
I want to water everything without asking.
The wind blows hard, delivering a whisper of *father.*

A silent, invisible yoke. You dream of morphine.
Another addiction, directing you to another sort of death.
But you say in the dream, *I have you and I don't want to die.*
Light against stone. The silence of a clenched muscle.

Some days I think I want to get married.
It's a matter of linguistics; I want to say *husband.*
By the Rio Chiquito, Catanya told me lobsters mate for life.
I thought of how many halves of couples I'd eaten.

I'm sorry; I was hungry. When we woke this morning,
we spoke without words of the wide, green field in the distance.
It was before the alarm went off, after the shrill of coyote.
Quick lightning split Pedernal.

It was more than the curve of your bent elbow, more
than the words we said that kept us together, more
than that particular intersection. We saw the fragile
leaf of the unflowering pansy and felt afraid.

A song is building inside the lining of our throats.

About the Author

Renée Gregorio was born in Wakefield, Massachusetts in 1955.
Years later, after earning an M.A. degree from Antioch University
in London, she moved to New Mexico. She lived in Taos for
several years, then outside Santa Fe, and recently relocated to
Albuquerque where she makes her home in Barelas.

She has worked as a bookstore manager, freelance book editor,
writer, and teacher as well as working as an editor for the New
Mexico state legislature. She has performed in "Dead Poet Bouts"
in New Mexico as well as been a member of the jazz/poetry
group, Luminous Animal. She was one of the founding editors of
the *Taos Review*.

Her first published poems appeared in *The Rialto* and *Writing
Women* in England during her time at Antioch. Since then,
poems have appeared across the U.S.—in *Iris, Exquisite Corpse,
Blue Mesa Review, Prairie Smoke, Fish Drum,* among others. She
also has published several shorter books of poetry. This is her
first full-length collection.

Other books by Renée Gregorio

The X Poems
(X Press, Santa Fe, NM)

When the Breathing Stops
(Yoo-Hoo Press, Farmington, NM)

Words Rising in the Dark Air
(Yoo-Hoo Press, Farmington, NM)

Circling Orgasmic
(12th Street Press, Providence, RI)

About Blinking Yellow Books

We are a non-profit press run by writers in Taos, New Mexico. Our guiding vision is to create a place where an alternative voice can emerge outside the constraints of commercial viability. This ongoing list of titles (an average of three per year) will continue to represent a diversity of style and experience linked by the essential thread of literary integrity.

Other Available Titles

Shine Boys *a story about Santa Fe*—by Vincent Younis.
  ISBN 1-883968-06-2, 120pp., paper, $10.00.
  (novella)

A House in Order—by Debbie McCann. Photos by Robert McCann.
  ISBN 1-883968-03-8, 128pp., paper, $10.00.
  (short stories)

Skeleton of a Bridge—by Robert Mirabal.
  ISBN 1-883968-02-X, 120pp., paper, $10.00.
  (stories)

A Little Book of Lies—by Phyllis Hotch. Drawings by Doris Fields.
  ISBN 1-883968-01-1, 36pp., paper, $6.00.
  (poems)

Upcoming in 1996

The Path through the Pillars—by Erik Kongshaug.
  ISBN 1-883968-07-0, 288pp., paper, $14.00.
  (novel)